M000268347

A LIVING SPACE

Kit Kemp
A LIVING SPACE

WORDS BY

KIT KEMP

WITH

FIONA McCARTHY

PHOTOGRAPHS BY

SIMON BROWN

hardie grant books
MELBOURNE · LONDON

oversized

texture →

Contents

Introduction

The idea behind this book, *A Living Space*, was actually first inspired by an exhibition of the same name I curated for Contemporary Applied Arts in 2010. Then, we wanted to find ways to excite and inspire people to work with the CAA's many talented artists, sculptors, textile designers and ceramicists, so we brought together whole room sets of specially commissioned pieces to show how a bespoke, highly personalised chest, vase or rug could instantly transform any living space. At that moment I realised how closely I held this bespoke sensibility to my heart, and how integral it had become to my own design process, whether it be for my own home or for one of the many hotels I co-own with my husband Tim, as part of Firmdale Hotels in London and New York. I suddenly felt that the idea of a book might be the ideal way to explore and explain this further for a wider audience.

In this book, I hope you will find a myriad of ideas and the encouragement to listen to your heart and trust your own instinct: I have one design rule and that is, there are no rules. If I can give you any advice, it is don't be afraid to give it a go. If someone comes in halfway through the design process and has an opinion contrary to yours, then send them away until you are done. And always remember to keep it personal – I would never have anything in our hotels that I wouldn't have in my own home. Design is a private, intimate process and you have to embrace the many twists and turns it takes to creating an exciting, inspiring but ultimately liveable space.

Through the ten chapters of this book, I hope you will see how colour, pattern, reclaimed and revamped old finds, customised furniture and fabrics, art and crafts, and unexpected, quirky details can make any interior special. I don't want to create a pastiche of the past, but instead find little touches – like using a kerosene can, instead of one in classically cut crystal, as a lamp base in a romantic bedroom – that make a room say 'now'. I always hope that in every interior I design, there is an element of something that anyone entering the room can relate to. Perhaps it triggers a nostalgic memory or simply tickles their fancy and makes them laugh.

It is a great compliment when someone comes into one of my hotels and asks 'Did you have to do very much here?' They don't realise that there wasn't actually a 'here' before we arrived. Oh what luxury to be able to work on buildings that are architectural gems! Instead, we usually start from scratch and turn often-neglected, derelict areas, like car parks and old warehouses, into regenerated, burgeoning new neighbourhoods – no mean feat when all you have to start with are ideas in your head, plans on paper and a hard-hat building site. The interior designer Mary Fox Linton once asked me how I work in this way – I told her that when I go to bed at night instead of counting sheep, I walk through all the corridors and rooms of the building in my mind, as it is the best way for me to try to understand it.

A great space need not be the most glamorous or luxurious – it is how personal and interesting you make it, how much it reflects you, your interests and your humour, that lends it a warm welcome. Great building bones are fantastic but not everything. For me, inspiration can come from everywhere – peering through the windows of people's homes whilst walking down a London street (the façades identical, yet each interior very different to the next), collecting textiles wherever I travel, remembering the colours of the sky at dusk whilst horse riding through the New Forest, or buying a piece of art because it reminds me of one of my daughters – which I hope in turn makes the pages in this book, the rooms in my hotels, and my belief in life that anything goes all the more inspiring for you.

A Stitch in Time

Some designers are led by their love of line and architecture, others by client relationships or the latest technologies. My inspiration comes from a love of fabrics, their texture, colour and tone, whatever age or geographical origin; they are very often the start of my creative process.

I see a fabric and just have to use it in some way, shape or form. I like to keep an open mind and see everything in the marketplace. I like to be aware of new processes, new designs, up-and-coming designers, and we all wait with great excitement the arrival of each season's new fabric collection. I am never happier than when sitting on the floor surrounded by reams of material, fabric swatches and pattern books – in fact, one of my earliest memories is of rooting through deep drawers in large chests full of stored materials that my mother had hoarded away. My team often joke that my office looks more like a junk shop, where it becomes nearly impossible to reach my desk for all the pieces of furniture that start to pile up, awaiting scrutiny and reupholstering in a newly-discovered textile gem.

I am constantly collecting fabrics on my travels – unique, often handcrafted fabrics that I know I won't find at home, and I use them in a number of ways, whether pulled across a canvas and hung on the wall or framed in perspex; or remnants used to create a series of cushions or patchwork throws. A delicate embroidered sampler, simply framed, becomes a work of art; South American blankets become upholstery for chairs and inspiration for a new rug's ranch-stripe design. I adore boiled wool as an upholstery, particularly when the seams are turned inside out and the selvedges finished in a constrasting coloured stitching.

Intricately embroidered and needlepointed fabrics are something I particularly cherish – I love the way textiles so often tell a story, conveying a history of the maker or capturing a moment in time that can be treasured forever in the intricate craftsmanship of these timeless, precious pieces.

PREVIOUS PAGE:
A bookcase at the Crosby Street Hotel was inspiration for my 'Bookends' fabric, designed with Christopher Farr, used on the chapter opening number.

If pressed to describe my style – something I never like to do because it seems to no longer allow for any change in the future – I would say it is carefree and colourful. My aim as a designer is to make surroundings a joyful thing – to bring in elements of intrigue and curiosity that create a sense of adventure and fun. This is not to be mistaken for gimmickry however – comfort and quality are at the core too.

The Six Senses of Design

Luxury design is such an abstract concept because the essence of what constitutes luxury is such a subjective, and ultimately personal, experience. For me, it is the antithesis of glitzy, shiny fabrics, ostentatious glamour and something that feels like a pastiche on the past. Instead, I design around stimulating and inspiring the senses.

SIGHT

The aspect of a room is key: I have never adhered to a style of design that looks like it has been 'painted by numbers'. I like to play up to the individuality of each room: the way the light bounces around it, the view outside its windows, the depth and breadth of its dimensions and proportions. Next, I think of colour, because for me, colour is everything. Solid hues, bold patterns, subtle undertones – it is what constantly inspires me and it is definitely never something to fear. I am constantly enthralled by how one can use and abuse it, and I mean this in a good way: there's no need to be precious about colour, in fact, be bold with it. That's when it works best. Trying to match it to the 'nth' degree can actually deaden an interior.

If access to natural light is limited, I try to embrace it rather than try to change it – darker, moodier hues and pattern can work to enliven the space. Where rooms have floods of light, I keep the colour scheme more simple and tonal, maximising the use of subtle textures to help bounce all that lovely daylight around the room.

I also introduce colour into a room through objects – one key piece can provide the perfect focal point in a room, and the ambience of the space can radiate out from it. Against a neutral backdrop, I like to throw in colour-dipped pieces of vintage furniture (from wooden chairs to sideboards and coffee tables), collections of luminescent glassware, or a generous armful of printed and embellished cushions. You'd be amazed how quickly it transforms a room into a happy oasis.

SOUND

When the window is open, the birds will sing, the trees will blow in the wind and the rain will patter against the windowpane. Each, in their own way, help to enhance the beauty of a space – but sometimes designing a room can be about eliminating the sound of traffic outside or the noise of a neighbour above or below. I love to see a bright red double-decker bus whizz by the window but I'd never want to hear it. Good window insulation and soft furnishings that absorb unwanted noise are essential to the harmony of any room.

Not all noises are negative – the sound of chic high-heels, clippity-clip-clipping on a wooden floor plays with the senses, evoking a sense of glamour and intrigue; but that same clippity-clip coming from every room in the house, or from the house next door, quickly loses its appeal. The rising crescendo of a party in full swing is great unless you want people to be able to sit, relax and have in-depth conversations of a very personal nature. I spend considerable time thinking about how each space will really be used, its level of foot traffic, how I want people to feel when they're in that space, and then use materials to enliven or soften the sense of noise bouncing around the room accordingly.

SMELL

Often it is the invisible things such as smell that creates a sense of true luxury in a space. I love the smell of soap suds, for example, and my idea of ultimate luxury is having bouquets of freshly-picked honeysuckle, jasmine, lavender or roses from the garden, warmed by the sunshine outside, to fill the air with delicious scent inside. Adding fragrance can have as much impact on how someone feels in a room as can the choice of furniture or wallpaper used.

Much like I love the powerful smell of wax-polished floors and furniture – the strong smell of a freshly French polished table in the Covent Garden Hotel feels so right for the mood of the space, as does the smell of freshly spruced leather or cowhide on the seats in the Soho or Charlotte Street Hotels. It brings the mood and ultimate experience of a room to fruition, and scent is often the thing you take away as the memory of a room, remembering it long after you've left it.

TASTE

Creating a dining space is all about stimulating both the taste buds and scintillating conversation. In a dining room – whether it be part of a large open-planned living and kitchen area, or an intimate room all of its very own – I always aim to create an environment where people want to sit, linger, enjoy, unwind. Dining spaces are no longer formal, foreboding rooms which are only used for special occasions.

A good dining chair is essential – comfortable, easy to manoeuvre and non intrusive (I prefer a low back which doesn't interfere with the eye's line of a room). Also, a handsome, simple table that can multi-task – homework, meetings, long lunches, grown-up dinners, letter writing, girlie nattering – is vital for accommodating the myriad of modern day demands expected of it. After all, today the kitchen/dining space is invariably the heart of the home – it is where everyone congregates, talks, nourishes and organises. It's certainly my favourite room in any house.

TOUCH

To me, the best interiors are those which infuse different textures and unexpected details within the room. Like rope or contrast-colour cording on chairs and ottomans, bold buttoning or intriguing skirting on sofas, mixed materials like marble or glass with metal legs on tables, and mixing up eras like fifties' modernist lines with bold batik or ikat prints (in the restaurant at Crosby Street Hotel, we teamed fifties' wallpaper and striking 'gum ball' bright plastic pendant lights alongside African ASAFO flags framed in perspex boxes).

Paper-backed fabrics instead of wallpaper are a wonderful way to absorb sound and lend a room an extra layer of warmth; and in areas like hallways, they

are practical too because they last forever. Objects on coffee tables or sideboards should be tactile and welcoming, in materials like wood, metal and clay, so that people are encouraged to embrace them and enjoy them, rather than live in fear of breaking them. *wood, metal, clay* If a guest's instinct is to want to reach out and touch everything they see, to explore and investigate, and to then smile in response, then I always feel as if I have created a successful interior. One of my key design mantras has always been 'never use a fabric you would not sit on in the nude'.

FUN

Finally, my sixth sense: a sense of FUN. I have always been drawn to things that are alive with wit and a bit of eccentricity – things that make me laugh. With each and every room I design, I want to peak people's curiosity. I encourage them to want to come in, to enjoy looking and poking around, to sit down, put their feet up, and never want to leave.

Little collections of mad objects, like childhood artworks, unusual figurines, or colourful ceramic pots, grouped together and encased in perspex can suddenly take on a whole new meaning and become an interesting and witty display of their own accord.

I love turning unusual objects – old kerosene cans, ceramic dogs – into lamps, and I've always fancied the idea of teaming a row of real stag heads with one made from cardboard interjected in the middle, pearls draped across its antlers. How fabulous can a series of botanical prints from an antique book, found inexpensively in a flea market, look when all framed in a group together on a wall? And nothing beats a pendant light crafted from something like organic pieces of smooth, ancient driftwood.

So much gets taken too seriously these days – I like to poke fun at those who try to dictate what we 'should and shouldn't have, should or shouldn't do', and I find that a humorous take on art is the perfect way to do this.

PREVIOUS PAGE:

One of my favourite moments is to sit down with a good book, while my husband, Tim, plays the piano – it is the collision of favourite colours, fabrics and artworks in this room which makes it one in which I am always happy to escape. It can be lovely with morning light but rather dark in the afternoon, so I used some bright colours and vivid patterns to jolly it up.

ABOVE:

I played with felt figures embroidered on green wool for covering armchairs and contrast stitching on the sofa.

OPPOSITE:

Robert Kime fabric made into curtains sits alongside a painting by Caroline McAdam Clark which is set against strips of old panels that I liked simply for their aged patina and pattern. In front, a lamp base made from an old decoy duck secured to a bread board has a lampshade made from an old Turkish ikat that brings the whole scheme together.

OVERLEAF, LEFT:

A needlepoint rug by The Rug Company makes for a surprisingly effective technicolour upholstery for a William IV-style chair, complete with shallow buttoning, offset by an intricately inlaid antique Spanish chest of drawers, a painting by Breon O'Casey and more antique ikat lampshades.

OVERLEAF, RIGHT:

A wall of raspberry red linen provides a dynamic background for a contrasting, tranquil painting – I love the way the red wall comes towards you but the painting provides a perspective that then carries you away, back into the distance. A large painting like this can make a small room appear much larger.

ABOVE:

'Suzani' and 'Wee Beasties' designs, from my embroidered fabric collection with Chelsea Textiles, are used on a blind and cushion (respectively).

OPPOSITE:

'Friendly Flowers', from the same collection, is used as a tablecloth.

ABOVE:

More of Chelsea Textiles are at play here. 'Hearts of Oak' works in perfect unison with this elaborately carved chair.

OPPOSITE:

A headboard covered in 'Mythical Beasts' complements the framed fairytale images on the walls.

For years I have been content to use the materials of other very talented designers and their teams, but recently I was approached by two design houses I really admire to create my own fabric collections. They are two very different companies, with no cross-over, and it has been a very satisfying process working with them both. Chelsea Textiles is known for its wonderful embroideries and attention to detail, and its colour and thread matching is second to none. I have known Mona Perlhagen and her daughter Jenny Simpson for more than twenty years, having used their fabrics throughout our hotels. My collection for them, centred around mythical beasts, dogs and the tribal Suzani print have a wonderful embroidered narrative to them which I hope captures a mood and the imagination.

My collection for Christopher Farr, better known for carpets than their exquisite range of fabrics, was a collaboration with Michal Silver. She was head designer at Mulberry when Roger Saul, who founded the label, was still running it, and knows exactly what she likes. This makes things easy for me because I tend to have an idea every week and she will say a definitive yes or no immediately. I wanted to create different weights of fabric for them because most of Michal's collections are on linen. I love linen but I am also mad about boiled wools for upholstery, whether it be sofas, chairs or ottomans.

'Bookends' was inspired by the zigzag of book spines on a bookshelf in Room 907 at Crosby Street – 'Willow' (inspired by a fabric collage by Pippa Caley) and 'Inside Out' (inspired by the detail of a painting we found in Paris) were created as a complement to this; I've also designed two jute rugs called 'Egg and Dart' and 'Pebbledash'. I have really enjoyed using them.

RIGHT:
'Bookends', 'Willow' and 'Inside Out' used to upholster chairs.

OVERLEAF:
Main picture, the walls, painted in Farrow & Ball's 'Ointment Pink', in Dorset Square's drawing room contrast well with 'Bookends' in pistachio.

OPPOSITE, FROM TOP LEFT CLOCKWISE:
We had the large armchairs designed and made with blanket stitching in a contrasting coral-coloured cotton; a beautifully carved mantelpiece teams with leather-bound scabbards set in a row; a sofa upholstered in an elegant embroidered Vaughan fabric, with felt piping and shallow-buttoned bottom cushions, sits below a collection of vintage cricketing illustrations; here I like the way the melange of different geometric fabrics mixed together for the curtains, cushion and chair.

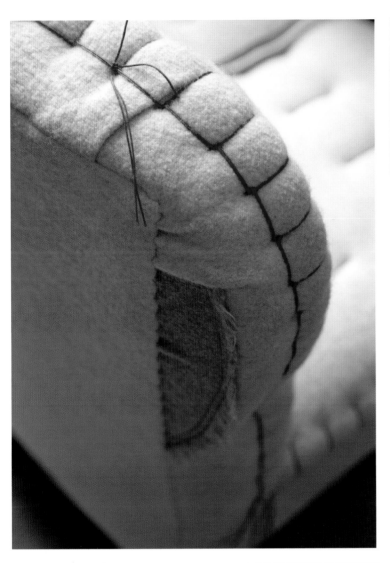

SERVICE

SERVICE

PREVIOUS PAGE:

The drawing room at the Covent Garden Hotel comes together in the detail. The wood panelling and intricate salvaged fireplace provide a neutral, natural backdrop for very brightly coloured silks, modern Suzanis and eighteenth-century embroideries and needlepoint.

The Canadian maple panelling comes from the old League of Nations building. It was one thing to purchase the panelling and quite another to put it into our building. It was quite a process and a tribute to our carpenters, Eddie in particular. There is something very satisfactory in renovating a building and knowing that it will look good for at least another hundred years. I know that building inside out, even down to the pigeon nesting outside the window in 304.

THIS PAGE, ABOVE:

A long-distance view of the drawing room, through to Tiffany's library, showing an unusual pointed pelmet that sits behind Designer's Guild silk curtains.

JANET HAIGH

JANET HAIGH
Suzy Cooper 1987

Embroidered samplers of famous female potters by Janet Haigh, including Susie Cooper (above) and Charlotte Rhead (left), were found at an auction tucked away in a folder, not being used to best advantage. Here, framing them has instantly elevated them into exquisite pieces of handiwork that you can admire and examine for hours.

PREVIOUS PAGE AND LEFT:

In the Terrace Suite at Soho, the curtain fabric made especially for us in India was the starting point of the room's design, along with the large patchwork sofas made in collaboration with Pippa Caley. The needlework and embroidery here are details you won't find anywhere else which makes it so unique. The Kasthall 'rag' rugs also lend a charming homemade feel.

ABOVE:

The gold leaf and aubergine details of the Carey Mortimer painting work with a chair covered in Neisha Crosland's flock linen 'Tudor Rose'. In the two rooms I worked with the same colours but in reverse so that each felt different, but could easily mix and match in mood.

ABOVE AND OPPOSITE:

I covered this headboard with an old Romeo Gigli scarf that I loved for its colours but it was too large to wear. It is perfect mixed up with a framed African embroidery sitting above the desk, a Kurdistan fabric used to cover the footstool, a pink velvet covered chair and beaded bed cushions.

THIS PAGE (AND PREVIOUS):

This room has a lot of Northern light, so to prevent it feeling too cold, layers of textures through felt embroidery and patterned fabrics make it feel warm for a countryside setting. I like raised fireplaces where you can store wood beneath the burning embers and the fireplace becomes the heartbeat of the room.

Bespoke and One-Off's

We are bombarded by television, magazines and the media with an overload of ideas, making it harder to surprise people; now it requires more thought to make that special space feel individual and your own. That's why creating a bespoke piece of fabric or having a piece of furniture tailor-made is such a satisfactory solution. It requires a lot of thought and collaboration, and an initial idea can transform into a very different visual experience because the creative process is organic and moves along with added ideas and minds in the process.

I love talking to artists and initiating an idea, but there is one key thing to always remember: choose your artist with care and when you have done so, let them get on to do the creating. It is too restraining for them if you are dictatorial about every little detail – an artist's best work is never done with someone looking over their shoulder. Give them space and look forward to being surprised by the final result.

Being original doesn't take much really. It is not about being clever, but rather, about listening to yourself and having enough confidence to see an idea through. Personally I like things to look a little home-made and I like colours to sing. It is what makes you look again.

PREVIOUS PAGE:

Bespoke miniature mannequins line a mantelpiece, and 'Willow' by Christopher Farr is featured on the chapter opening number.

OPPOSITE:

A set of Frederik Färg chairs, striking with their covers of ruffled industrial felt, complement the gritty folds of slate in Tom Stogdon's custom-made table and Carol Sinclair's sculpture of huge turned pieces of Welsh slate.

When designing the entrance lobby of the Haymarket Hotel, on one side I hung a very large modern black and white painting by English artist John Virtue against a modern black sofa and vibrant yellow chairs, all underpinned by a Marni rug. On the other side, I have a 22-foot-long installation of tiny stones by Sue Lawty, teamed with an eighteenth-century Swedish sofa and two bergères, underpinned by a second Marni rug. In the centre sits a liquid steel sculpture by Tony Cragg which unites the two very different sides of the lobby. These are all very disparate pieces but they balance well with one another and look good. I don't like matching many things in pairs – to begin with, pairs are always more expensive, and it's so much easier to find one nice table and use it rather than try to match or copy it. Instead, playing with dissimilar things at similar heights maintains a sense of symmetry.

This room, 303 at Covent Garden, is the
perfect example of how bespoke details make
a room feel truly unique. I worked closely
with the talented textile and carpet designer
Christine Van Der Hurd – the ultimate
colourist in my opinion – to create the fabrics
in this room, from the furniture and walls
to the bedhead and rugs. We have a great
working relationship where she asks what
colours I am thinking of using and suddenly,
she comes out with a flow of ideas for every
part of the room. The combination of the
exquisite needlepoint used on the armchairs
and cushions, teamed with the simple
cross-stitch on the back of the dining chairs,
is lovely. Where else could you get such
quality of workmanship? It feels like these are
precious pieces that you might never
see again.

Flora and foliage is another important element we use to create a unique feel to a room: we have long collaborated with Stephen Wicks and Mark Welford, two former Royal Ballet dancers, who now run Bloomsbury Flowers. I like the way they incorporate unexpected elements like these container vases here (below the fairy painting), where they've wrapped them in bark and string. It simply lends another unexpected, dynamic textural element to the room. I've never liked spikey, exotic flowers arrangements – I like flowers to be in season, as if just picked and bought in from the garden.

LEFT:
An old oil painting in a gild frame sits above a console table made from an old piece of furniture to which we have added a brilliant white wooden top. It creates a nice contrast with the pair of Gareth Devonald Smith lamps.

In the lobby, by the lifts at the Soho Hotel, Charlie Wells' tubes of colour and a wing chair covered in an old Suzani fabric (with its back and sides covered in a black felt) sit behind an oval painting by Joe Fan, originally meant to hang on a wall but instead turned into a table with a clear top and base of bright red perspex.

OPPOSITE:
A Roger Cecil painting sits above a set of two Ashley Cartwright benches which have been stacked one on top of the other to create an interesting shelf.

The curiosity aspect of the sitting room at Number Sixteen is what makes this room so interesting. The lamp of coloured perspex discs we designed with Charlotte Packe sits beside Allyson Reynolds' paintings of vibrant moths. Underneath an old driftwood chandelier we hung some little birds and, for a bit of fun, framed an old pair of Gucci heels, sitting on AstroTurf, in a perspex box.

My collaboration with Althea Wilson, in commissioning the fabric used here for these curtains in the drawing room at Knightsbridge, led to the creation of the miniature mannequins (seen at the start of this chapter and page 61).

My design schemes are often influenced by random things I notice wherever I go. The thought process behind the colour and pattern scheme in this room was actually inspired by some catwalk images I spotted from Paris fashion week one year, where there was a mood of gentle greys set against an odd combination of circles and patchwork. It worked so brilliantly on the clothes, I thought it would create an interesting dynamic in a drawing room as well.

Abstract painting by John Illsley (one of the founding members of Dire Straits, now a well-regarded modern painter in his own right).

wooden mushrooms on base

At the other end of the Knightsbridge Hotel drawing room, an illuminated ladder stands against a very simple bookcase to add interest. In the middle hangs a painting by Breon O'Casey; in front sits a carver chair upholstered in an Althea Wilson fabric created specially for the room.

Extending the upholstery of the sofa down over the legs and feet provides a tailor-made, personalised touch.

Customising the edges of a fender with leather is a clever way to ensure the ends don't start to fray too soon, but it also adds a smart finish to the fabric.

LEFT:

Althea Wilson created these miniature mannequins for me, inspired by paintings and fabrics I was going to use for The Knightsbridge (which opened in 2002). I loved it when they were delivered as she had been inspired to give each one a little hat as well. These, and the full-size custom-covered mannequins, which have become a signature detail in every bedroom of our hotels, lend another decorative, sculptural element to a room.

BELOW:

A bespoke piece is created out of reupholstering an old wing chair in a combination of an ethnic-inspired fabric and plain linen.

OPPOSITE:

OPPOSITE:

A bespoke Rupert Williamson moving set of drawers is made of ash and oak. All the drawers open up and swing out independently, the perfect spot for storing socks and hot-water bottles at the top of a stairwell.

ABOVE:

Justine Smith's 'Street' letters, made for us out of assorted American coins, teams with a set of Peter Blake alphabet letter collages at Crosby Street.

The artist Alexander Hollweg created a modern-day mural for Oscar, the restaurant in the Charlotte Street Hotel. It depicts everyday scenes of modern life, inspired by a photograph of an original mural by Duncan Grant of very elegant ladies coming out of a London Underground station, which we saw in a 1912 issue of *Illustrated London News*. In our murals, you can see details like the London Eye, people on mobile phones, at the cinema, and my husband Tim playing chess, but created in the style and colour palette of the Bloomsbury Set.

Inside Out

Bringing the scale of outside to inside is important. I have always preferred a heftier scale. I don't like fiddly tables and things to trip over. I much prefer a weighty table with a marble top that could also be used outdoors. Bringing it inside brings a scale and grandeur to a room.

Some people prefer silver or ormolu, I prefer wood and slate. It doesn't have to be rustic but I think robust is a better word. Mixing in robust makes the exquisite look even more beautiful. A silver birch wood box covered in moss with several exquisite lily of the valley plants in flower, sitting on an early Swedish fossil stone table, really works.

I admire the work of Carol Sinclair. Her massive wooden cones that she calls 'pyro' forms bring an extraordinary presence to a conservatory or inside/outside space. If you do use strong organic forms you need space around them to breathe.

Simple things like teaming a lamp with a basket-work shade will cast welcoming shadows on walls and ceilings. I bought some very large terracotta pots and had them zinc-welded together to make a tower. It looks very effective, our own attempt at Brancusi.

A broken marble bust or small sculpture found on your travels will instantly transform and become the focal point of a room if placed on a centre or side table. I also often use the term 'inside out' for the stitching on some of our furniture. We turn the seaming inside out and finish the selvedges in contrasting coloured stitching. This looks good with the boiled wools I love to use.

Using very contrasting materials can be effective too. We made a glorious sepia oak table with pebbles running down the whole length of the centre of the table, but the interest too is in the legs which have been made from strengthened glass. It works in old and new interiors and holds its own – I have found that this works especially well in hallways, entrances or garden rooms where the boundaries of inside/ outside are more easily blurred.

OPPOSITE:
A Swiss antique table with elaborate, cylindrical carving and lustrous patina looks out across the iconic water-towered skyline of downtown Manhattan at the Crosby Street Hotel.

Creating a luscious wildflower meadow outside the doors of the Meadow Suite at Crosby Street was one of the unexpected delights of designing a hotel in New York. We had to lift two feet of soil up to the second floor to create this wildflower terrace garden, which guests of the room can walk around to their heart's content. It's the last thing you imagine to find in the heart of a big, bustling city, and it links beautifully with the theme of the hotel's rooftop garden where we grow our own produce to be used in the kitchens and to house four Chilean Araucana chickens – Brooklyn, Manhattan, Queens and Bronx – who kindly deign to provide fresh eggs when they feel like it. It truly feels as if it has been here forever, which is all the more amazing given the reality that the hotel is brand new, built between two existing buildings on a car park in 2010. All of this helped us to scoop a GOLD LEED Green Building award in the process (the only one to be awarded in NYC at the time).

Here, I've played with the textures of nature and a palette of gentle taupes, greens and browns to help bring the 'outside in' to the Meadow Suite bedroom. To be able to bring the feeling of the countryside into such an urban environment is very comforting.

HEADBOARD/MANNEQUIN: A bold floral print on a dark olive green background covers the headboard, paired with matching beaded-edge cushions and mannequin, to accentuate the room's mood of a blooming garden. Teamed with a soft linen on the walls, the overall effect really gives the room a rich 'chlorophyll' punch.

FOOTSTOOL: A footstool in a pretty hand-embroidered fabric is the perfect way to use a little of a beautiful, but expensive, material to great effect. I've always felt the whole point of staying in one of our hotels is to experience a sense of something unique and individual, and using special fabrics like this lends a one-off touch.

DESK: The desk lamps, made for us in India, lend a shimmering tactility to the room.

CURTAINS: The striking geometric fabric lends the floral fabric a modern edge so the overall effect is dramatic rather than chintzy.

This magnificent front
door looked rather
old-fashioned with
a painted finish and
dimpled glass. Sanding
it back to its natural
original bronze and
inserting sandblasted
glass felt more
contemporary. In the
hallway, a beautiful
old flagstone floor was
reinstated because it
was hiding underneath
carpet. The doorway to
the drawing room was
moved across so that it
lined up directly with
the front door and the
back garden. It is a
great luxury to maximise
the sense of light
inside a house and to
be able to look directly
through to the greenery
of the garden.

ABOVE:

Two sides of a hallway play with elements of the 'outside': an old mud beehive provides a sculptural element alongside a limed chest of drawers by Julian Chichester and an antique Swedish mirror with an anchor as its emblem.

OPPOSITE:

A bold but simple flower painting and a set of four Anna Raymond paintings, with a chair covered in a reclaimed piece of fabric, give the space a zing of neon. In the corner, the spade used to dig the first footings for the foundation at Crosby Street, a gift from our architects in New York, sits by the front door.

OPPOSITE:

At Crosby Street, near the entrance to the restaurant, an *étagère* arrangement of plants and stone sculpture lends to the 'inside out' mood of the welcoming lobby.

ABOVE:

A cane-backed *conversationé* chair in the lobby of the Covent Garden Hotel leads the eye towards a dramatic curtain, made from needlepoint rugs, which creates a theatrical entrance to the reception area.

The silky smooth bronze Botero cat welcomes guests to the Charlotte Street Hotel, sitting in front of a Bloomsbury-inspired rug and a pair of antique leather chairs. The top of his head has been worn through the blackened bronze in some places because everyone loves to touch him like a talisman for good luck.

I often lug benches that have sat for years in the garden into a hallway, upon which I then sit bunches of flowers, hats and coats. Wood or metal benches, if they are the right scale, look good if they are sitting on wooden floorboards, flagstones or even chequered marble (but not on carpet), and they can withstand pots of flowers on them without doing too much damage to the surface of the bench.

CLOCKWISE:

Pebbles are set into a wooden bench; I added a mobile below the chandelier to create the effect of looking into the centre of a watery pool – the crystals glow and the shapes look like water lilies. A chair is upholstered with an Argentinean blanket, with deep buttoning and a leather handle to finish.

LEFT:

Corners can often be dark and unloved spaces so they need to be filled with interest and illumination. I've done this here with a mix of striking wooden forms, an old chimney pot and metal bath filled with flowers, behind which hidden uplighters create the most beautiful shadows at night.

PREVIOUS PAGE AND RIGHT:

The colours and stripes of Argentinean blankets were the inspiration for this room, from the upholstery on the dining room chairs to the rug below the table which I designed for The Rug Company. I like the way the colours feel worn and very robust.

The composition of a new bench, painted in Designers Guild 'Tuscan Olive', placed below a window and between two worn stone sculptures, makes a new patio look naturally worn and weathered.

My favourite room, at home
in London, is this kitchen.
We decided to turn what was
originally the best room in the
house, the very large sitting
room, into the kitchen, thanks
to a suggestion by Robert Kime.
It faces the garden and teamed
with a conservatory, it became
our dining room where we now
spend most of our time.

Blousey pink florals by Bennison and a wooden sculpture mounted on pink perspex add a dash of brightness to the elegant conservatory space.

LEFT:

An intriguing tablescape in the dining area, with old copper and Paola Navone 'plaster of Paris' watering cans, painted bronze figures by Ramiro Fernandez Saus and a beaded zebra from Africa.

OPPOSITE:

I have used an intriguing light sculpture by Gareth Devonald Smith (above) in a newly built back extension of a country house. I like the contrast of such a contemporary chandelier against the elegance of the carved solid oak staircase – he works in a wonderful scale, with a very different take on the organic and found materials he uses. This unexpected combination makes you take a second glance as you travel up and down the stairs.

Antique With Modern

Artwork and furniture date and can look very unfashionable as time goes by, but the good pieces usually survive. It could just be a wonderful patina of wood, waxed and polished to perfection, or a painting that tells a story. Memories of staying at Granny's and living with her ticking grandfather clock become precious and so, as an adult, even though our pad might now be super modern, when we come across a clock with the face of the moon and hands that look like Red Admiral's wings we cannot resist it. It is often the quirky, unusual pieces that suddenly create the character in a living space.

It seems a shame to create an uncompromisingly modern interior when your home is a nineteenth-century country cottage with bumpy walls and a low ceiling. Equally, why stuff your high-rise eyrie with 100 per cent antique furniture? In other words, the architecture will dictate what feels comfortable. That is not to say that it cannot be your own individual 'take' on the period and your own concept of style. It is fun to take an antique chair and cover the front in a striking modern zebra print or make a patchwork out of favourite pieces of vintage fabric and cover a sofa in it; I actually made the patchwork sofas at Crosby Street with a good friend of mine, Louise Hallet – we played seventies' music for a week while I chopped and she sewed. I really feel like I am a part of those sofas.

In Brasserie Max, my favourite nineteenth-century painting of fishermen's wives mending their nets, and a young woman looking sad with longing for her husband to return from the sea (seen on the previous page), sits happily beside a Juliette Losq work that was painted in 2010 and depicts a watery view over a many-layered bridge. Their scales are similar and against the greeny-bronze walls they give enormous interest to evening drinkers and morning porridge-eaters alike.

PREVIOUS PAGE:
'Mythical Beasts' fabric designed for Chelsea Textiles' embroidery collection used on the chapter opening number.

OPPOSITE:
An old French writing desk and vintage ceramics mix with modern fabrics by Colefax & Fowler and Galbraith & Paul.

I have created a modern take on fabrics and decorating within this traditional room. I have mixed Dominque Keiffer ribbed pink corduroy with blue piping, bright floral printed curtains and cushions, finished with a Designers Guild pearlised shell trim. On the floor a traditional Turkish rug brings the whole look together.

OPPOSITE:

A mix of old and new, with embroidered 'Milas' linen fabric by Vaughan, abstract painting, a modern mirror (inlaid with a narrow double strip of perspex which gives the appearance of an old Irish mirror), and a lucite lamp sitting on a traditional rosewood table.

ABOVE:

Alongside a rosewood octagonal table and sixties' lucite lamp hangs a modern painting by Mark Entwisle from Long & Ryle. I bought this the same year Anthony Gormley exhibited his huge lightbox installation at the Hayward Gallery in London in 2007 – I loved the magical idea of a child entering a lightbox in the middle of an English wood.

Given its London location, the Charlotte Street Hotel is my tribute to the Bloomsbury Set. Here, Vanessa Bell painted panels set the mood, along with an antique wing chair covered in a modern fabric and leather piping, rough wooden planters and a Bloomsbury-inspired rug. The walls are actually made from MDF, made to look like expensive panelling with the feel that they have been there for ages, which they simply have not.

It seemed appropriate to hang one of Roger Fry's works as he was the main protagonist of the Bloomsbury movement and the one responsible for bringing the first Post-Impressionist exhibition to London (where amazingly the paintings were sneered at). It's only a small, rather simple painting, but it is the imposing contemporary frame we had made to go around it which makes it look more important.

This is the drawing room at Crosby Street, opening out to the sculpture garden – with 22-foot-high ceilings and a long, narrow scale, it needed to be broken up into three separate areas. We did this by adding two Gothic-style fireplaces with large contemporary paintings by Bard above at either end, and a lovely old butcher's block table in the middle. To the left, a Rolf Sachs' 'Light Chemistry' modern lamp sits on a carved wooden table, in front of an imposing scrollwork mirror. To the right, the long narrow recess is filled by a limed table and a collection of framed prints.

A wooden Filipino totem sculpture, originally a gate post and said to ward away the evil spirits, adds height on a side table and casts a protective presence around the room.

OPPOSITE:

The strong, primitive paintings, constructed almost like collages, by the artist Mimmo Paladino, and the roughly hewn contemporary pot, provide a strong focal point.

ABOVE:

A striking modern contrast is created with this cartoonish 'kapow'-shaped canvas wall sculpture. It's not often you have enough space to hang something like this.

Compare and Contrast

Black against white, or magenta against yellow, contrast so completely that they actually complement one another and show each other to best advantage. In Room 1007 at Crosby Street we have used a deep aubergine linen on the walls and contrasted it with brilliant white to make a lively background to the furniture. Stripped light oak works well here too with a variety of contrasting fabrics. You would think that this would make a rather jarring and busy scheme but the feeling is one of calm and luxury.

Very often a room requires a hefty piece of almost ugly furniture to pull it all together. I found this massive old marquetry roll-top desk, made in Japan for the European market in the nineteenth century, and it is the pièce de résistance in the large panelled drawing room. Many people say they do not like antiques but I feel they draw the most attention in any room; people love to touch them and discover their secrets. Contrast this desk with a very contemporary, streamlined John Stefanidis chair, an eighteenth-century Swedish clock and a mid-twentieth-century telephone and it all looks surprisingly as if it has been there forever.

It is fun to surprise – a copy of the Mona Lisa wearing spotted sunglasses contrasted against the bone inlay of a chest of drawers, or the teaming of a houndstooth check against a Syrian table, or a bold Neisha Crosland flower print on an easy chair under the subtle tones of a Carey Mortimer painting.

I like to live with rooms and see them in every season and every light, whether it be brilliant sunshine or the deepening gloom of thunder and lightning. It gives me the chance to compare and contrast the the colours, the fabrics, the architectural details and textures, the aspect. And quite often, I start again.

PREVIOUS PAGE:
Swaffer 'Parterre' used on the chapter opening number and a mix of Etro and Christine Van Der Hurd fabrics with Abbott & Boyd trim.

ABOVE:

In the drawing room at Covent Garden, a vintage French children's horse-and-cart toy sits below a maple-framed naïve dog painting.

OPPOSITE:

One of my mum's old tapestry-covered chairs sits next to a fruitwood table, underneath what is called an old 'cartoon' – this is the name used to describe the canvas patterns embroiderers follow, complete with little numbers, to guide the colour of the different threads when creating a tapestry.

The odd but dramatic mix of Catherine Cuthbert's unusual ceramics and an extraordinary mother-of-pearl console table (with an arch that looks like the mouth of a cave) contrasts with the graphic texture of a Bard painting. Those lovely grainy feet felt perfect for the Crosby Street Hotel, hanging opposite the lift with the lovely association of the footprints our guests make on their global journeys.

At the Crosby Street Hotel, an enveloping deep aubergine linen on the walls contrasts with a pale limestone fireplace, white modern chandelier and candelabra, and washed-out woods. Here, a compare and contrast mood is built up with layers of Bennison linens, Mulberry paisleys and Etro tweeds, perspex-framed pieces of Indian sari fabric, and intricately turned wooden table legs.

FROM TOP LEFT, CLOCKWISE:

A room with a dramatic view.

A white frame against the aubergine background looks clean and contemporary. The geometric pattern of the curtains contrasts yet complements the floral pattern of the headboard.

Even though the chandelier is large, to suit the proportions of the room, the wirework construction gives it a lightness and transparency.

A close-up detail of the intricate mirror (opposite, bottom left).

This candelabra is really just a bit of old junk and weighs a ton, but it's an unexpected detail in a modern bedroom. A few cherubs never did any anyone harm, in my opinion.

Deep-buttoned Etro houndstooth against aubergine linen is full of movement and vibrancy.

The intricate edge of a black and gild mirror sits on a table made from a mix of a marble top and an old metal balustrade base.

Same room, two different moods: a masculine, monotone black-and-white
scheme with houndstooth check on the sofa contrasts dramatically with the
vibrant multi-coloured Manuel Canovas, Jane Churchill and Lee Jofa fabrics
used opposite. One is tailored, the other is colourful and ethnic-inspired.

OVERLEAF, FROM TOP LEFT, CLOCKWISE:

Curtains and mannequin in prints from African Sketchbook, in colours made especially for us, teamed with fabrics by Kradvat and Stefanidis.

Pinstripe tailoring on walls and a houndstooth check on chair works with a perspex-framed Mona Lisa in sunglasses and mother-of-pearl inlaid chest-of-drawers.

A green linen wall is the backdrop to paisley print curtains and a graphic, geometric-shaped framed print.

Mad polka dots team with an old Dutch-style painting and purple velvet chair.

Against the clash of patterns in unusual tones of grey, the plain white bed offers a calm contrast to the headboard.

The plain red headboard makes the vibrant pattern of the wall really pop with colour.

ABOVE:

A traditional-shaped headboard is given a modern lift with Robert Allen fabric and silver studding.

LEFT:

This is a very tailored and yet easy look, with fresh white curtains relieving the greyness of the suiting-style fabric on the walls. On the sofa, using the same fabric in opposing colour ways is perfect for creating an unexpected but interesting contrast.

Here, a basement lobby needed pictures to act as a view so we sent the hyperrealistic artist Peter Rocklin from his studio in Yorkshire to New York to sketch Manhattan scenes.

OPPOSITE:
He captures SoHo moments like traffic lights and the iconic sign above Fanelli's Cafe on Prince Street.

BELOW:
The vivid purple and yellow of Peter's painting of my daughter Min, in strident mode, connects with the colour of the cinema next door. The painting was initially destined for the gym but didn't make it as it looked so good here.

Nature and Organic

Living with two elder brothers in a tiny house called Chaddlewood, Netley Firs Road, Hedge End, you can imagine what a tomboy I became. I could climb trees, jump between haystacks, and leap over stiles as well as all the boys, and would walk and cycle miles every day. That's where my love of the fresh air and countryside comes from. We could catch a bus to school but very often we would cut through the woods and Farmer Candy's fields to the sandpits and down to the churchyard to explore the gravestones. The lichen and moss that covered the stones in the long grass was beauty in itself, and the colours taught us the way they can combine and harmonise. If ever in doubt just look at nature and be assured of your choice of tone and colour.

There is nothing like the feel and look of a beautiful piece of wood. The patina developed by wax and love and care over years is irreplaceable. What's more, there are woods that are hard to come by these days, like walnut, many fruitwoods and even elm or sycamore, which are all the more valuable and covetable as a result. These woods really evoke the senses and bring to life memories of sliding across waxed oak floorboards in our socks when we thought no one was looking.

Bringing nature and organic pieces into the home is one of my favourite ways of grounding a room, making it feel comfortable rather than grand. These pieces lend an instant tactility and familiarity, easing their way into a room through tone and texture that works no matter what the age or style, formality or informality, of the space.

PREVIOUS PAGE:

A tapestry weave in organic colours used on the chapter opening number, lichens on old stone.

OPPOSITE:

Crystal ball and smooth stone base sits on a marquetry chest-of-drawers.

In the Townhouse at the Haymarket Hotel, the proportions of the John Nash-designed house attached to the hotel allowed us to play with the exquisite elegance of detail from the building's past, but by working with a fresh, bright colour and pattern palette, it made the interiors bold enough to feel right for now.

FRAMING FABRIC: I love to collect fabrics – old, new, embroidered or silk-screened – from around the world, and sometimes I frame them in perspex to hang on a wall, such as here with this Moroccan textile. It is far too beautiful to be packed away and lends another element of textured colour to the room.

FLOWERS: These are simple wirework candlesticks which we've dressed up for a special occasion with balls of moss and flowers. An instant way to add a sense of celebration.

INSIDE OUT STITCHING: I love the classic shape of this sofa, it's very bookish – the kind of sofa you would expect to find an Oxford don to be sitting on – and yet it is also very comfortable and supportive; it's also not too high-backed, so when it sits in the centre of a room, it doesn't break the flow. Showing the stitched seams of the upholstery, contrasted with a generous piping, stops it from feeling old-fashioned.

DADOS: I like to use a dado, or chair, rail to create a natural distinction between colour on the wall above and a neutral hue below, rather than continuing the colour the whole way down to the floor. This is a great way to provide a calm background against which you can team colour in furniture and rugs.

STYLING: Styling brings a room to life – here we've mixed together many elements of nature and yet it still feels sophisticated and appropriate for a city townhouse. The room itself is quite formal so these elements lend a quiet humanity: a decorative inlaid ivory box sits on a table made from reclaimed parquet flooring, and wooden shoe lasts and grain scoops in well-worn woods gleam with a history of use.

A sculptural candlestick with a piece of coral attached to it makes for an interesting shape in the room and an unusual reflection in the mirror – you see something different each time you look at it. It also works beautifully with the colours of the marble fireplace.

I always sit curtains well back from the window reveals so that every ounce of natural light can come into the room. Here, to play with the light and lend the room a shimmer, the leading and bottom edges of the natural linen curtains are given some tactile glamour with pearl beading and a double strip of coloured silk.

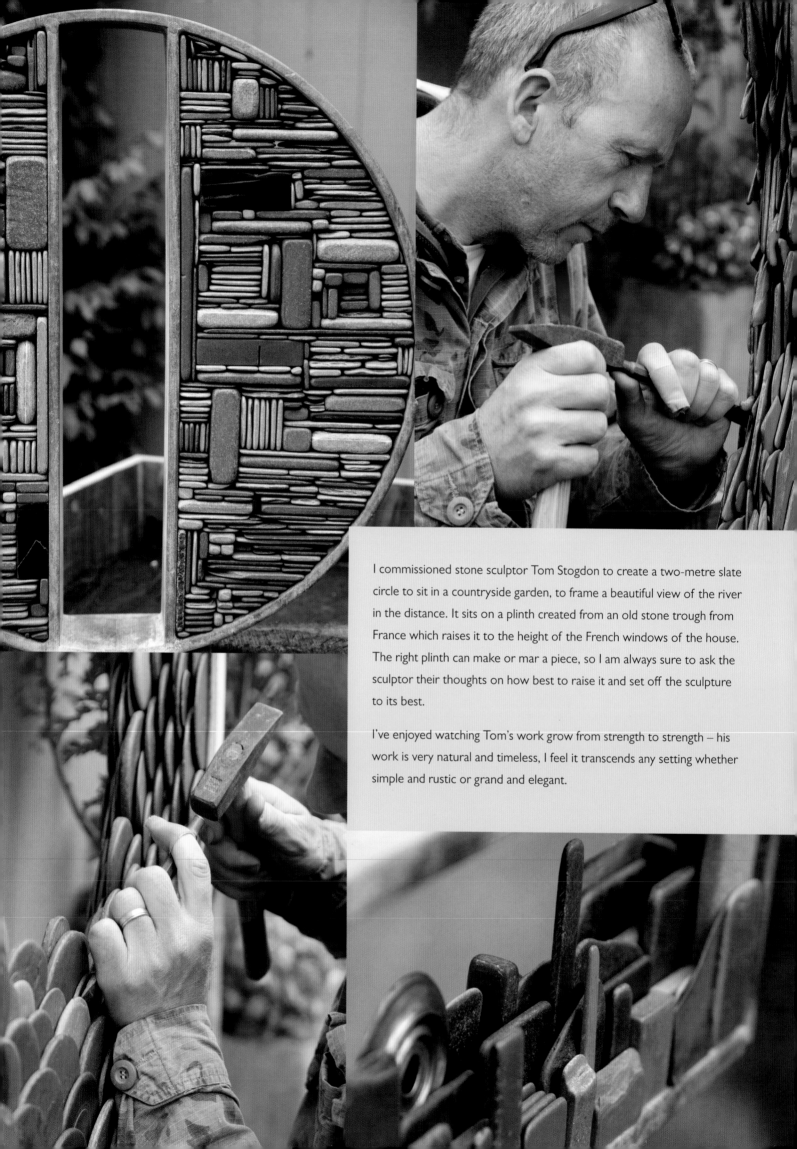

I commissioned stone sculptor Tom Stogdon to create a two-metre slate circle to sit in a countryside garden, to frame a beautiful view of the river in the distance. It sits on a plinth created from an old stone trough from France which raises it to the height of the French windows of the house. The right plinth can make or mar a piece, so I am always sure to ask the sculptor their thoughts on how best to raise it and set off the sculpture to its best.

I've enjoyed watching Tom's work grow from strength to strength – his work is very natural and timeless, I feel it transcends any setting whether simple and rustic or grand and elegant.

Nestling in an untidy flower bed, three birdbaths made from pottery and wood by Sarah Walton add a sculptural presence and height to the area (as the garden grows and matures) that works in all seasons.

This old olive press has been transformed into a natural water feature which provides a gentle dribble, rather than a gush, of water that sinks down into the stones below – I like that it looks as if it has been there for a long time. It provides something of interest as guests arrive at the house, and the cobblestones surrounding it echo the stones used in the stable block nearby.

An old tree root has been transformed into a bench, on top of which sits a seed box of fragrant thyme, which helped to make a new addition to a house look old.

OPPOSITE:

I found an old door knocker of a horse's head which I used to provide a focal point to the door, from which I hung bits of collected driftwood threaded on a string. It lends a lovely 'found' feel, creating a bit of character to detract away from the fact that this is a brand new extension and door. A really good French polisher, who knows how to create worn-in colours, is also invaluable.

In a new extension, very oversized oak beams help to transform the roof space into an interesting feature of its own accord. I brought in an old scull of a boat and perched it between the beams, the peeling paint of its hull just discernible, lending an instant warmth and interest to the room. A mix of blue and white from ceramic jars and China Seas fabric lends to the nautical theme.

OVERLEAF:

To complete the scheme, an old chandelier has been glued with shells. It really isn't big enough for the room but I don't mind. I like the fact that it is home-made and also compliments the old shell-covered table.

OPPOSITE:

Heather Jansch uses driftwood, metal and car filler to create sculptures of wild horses and deer. Here, we have one nestled in the birch trees at the bottom of the garden to compete with the real deer who wander in freely to nibble on our rosebuds. I like to place points of interest around a space to encourage people to get out and explore – the deer at the bottom of the garden draws you down there and makes you really have a good look around and enjoy the changing seasons.

ABOVE:

A necklace made up of charming tactile trinkets and a rope of wooden weights brings an organic touch to a simple Bella Figura lamp that sits by a sofa.

In the sculpture garden at Crosby Street, New York, organic pieces lend an inner-city location a rustic feel.

Mirrors set into driftwood frames enlarge the sense of space, concrete tabletops look like slices of an ancient tree, a Far Eastern bench boasts intricate wood carving, and terracotta pots are welded together with zinc to create sculptural pillars.

Dogs

I don't think a home is a home without a dog stretched out in front of the fire or sitting beside us when we are having a cup of tea. Somehow, our dogs do start to resemble us, in the way they look or the speed with which they move. Watch a very old person walking down the street, for instance, and it's guaranteed that their dogs will be moving sedately alongside them at the same speed. I know I have a more satisfactory conversation with my dog sometimes than I do with my husband or children. What's more, he even wags his tail and agrees with me. Dogs bring you down to earth, and a walk with my dogs really helps to put a particular situation into perspective.

As they make me laugh, with their amusing antics and funny expressions, I am always drawn to doggy paintings and anything associated with them. When I started to think about the design scheme for the Crosby Street Hotel in New York's SoHo area, I first began with cerebral ideas of creating a kind of salon for creative people, with 'art inspired by the written word' as its underlying ethos; yet the reality of all that high-mindedness is that 'dogs' quickly came into the picture.

When my team and I finally arrived in New York to open the hotel in the early summer of 2010, I asked two of my design assistants Flora and Stuart to go out onto the downtown streets to photograph all the local dogs of SoHo. I had this vision of fabulous high heeled shoes and dogs on leads at their feet, all photographed from the knees down; sadly I hadn't realised that New Yorkers tend only to wear flip flops on their feet in the summer so my idea of exotic footwear didn't show itself in our photographs. Still, we captured some great images which we hung in the hotel's lifts for the guests to look at while rising upwards to their floors.

Now people barely mention my Jaume Plensa ten-foot, round head sculpture or my Anselm Kiefer artwork. They only notice the presence of dogs in the form of artworks or Justine Smith's sculptures of dogs, made from copies of old *Beano* comics, that amiably greet guests in the lobby on arrival.

PREVIOUS PAGE:
'Moondog' fabric designed for Chelsea Textiles used on the chapter opening number, and the lobby at Crosby Street in New York.

ABOVE, FROM CLOCKWISE:

A chic cardboard box found in Biarritz made into a bed for our tabby, Tatty.

Dogs pop up anywhere in my design schemes – here an old painting of lovely dogs sits in my bedroom.

My doggies happily at home.

A stone dog keeps watch in the garden.

OPPOSITE:

Here, I love the combination of flowers, dog and carved wooden bull hall-chair together.

ABOVE:

My Suzani design for Chelsea Textiles, in large repeat on the curtains and a matching fabric on the chair, which has also been quilted to make it stronger, has been teamed with a natural check on both the underside and back of the chair.

OPPOSITE:

A favourite Staffordshire ceramic dog has been made into a lamp base.

The Haymarket Hotel's restaurant and bar is called Brumus, named after one of our beloved black and tan spaniels. Here we play with dog-shaped appliqués on the back of dining chairs and bar stools... and we have fun with a little game for visiting children — they have to hunt for the silhouette of the original Brumus, which is stitched onto the back of one of the chairs.

Dogs on walls and cushions in the lobby at Knightsbridge.

At home, the dogs have commandeered the best armchair so it is covered in a colourful rug that can be washed frequently. We chose our architect because he said he couldn't understand anybody who didn't love the smell of wet dog – from that moment I knew we would get on like a house on fire.

Four collages by Peter Clark. I was instantly captivated by his work when I stopped by Rebecca Hossack's gallery in Charlotte Street one day – it is witty and amusing and I never tire of it.

ABOVE:

A simple series of doggie postcards are made into a framed collection.

OPPOSITE:

At Covent Garden, a painting of gun dogs by a Scottish artist looks appropriate teamed against the drawing room's wooden panelling and silk curtains.

ABOVE:
An Indian wooden dog provides a sculptural presence in a room at
Crosby Street.

OPPOSITE:
A Scottie dog collage called 'Locks of Air', complete with a stamp
for a nose.

As we built the Crosby Street Hotel from scratch, we decided to run a little film on our website to show
how it progressed. I remember my first visit to Crosby Street when our site was just a car park and the
street was bumpy and cobbled. I saw a man who must have been seventy-years-old riding a butcher's bicycle
with purple hair and his dog, wearing a goat's bell on his collar, jingling along beside him as they both made
their way down the road. It was the last thing I expected to see in sophisticated New York. After that, I
started to notice lots of other coiffed and cared-for dogs and wondered where on earth they could be living.
Quite possibly on the 44th floor of a building.

Locks of Air   PeterClark 2001

Art and Collections

Art serves as one of my biggest inspirations but I treat art in public spaces quite differently from art in the home. Art in a lobby or public space has to be arresting, even to the most unobservant person. To stop a busy businessman on his way to a meeting or someone who is jetlagged and grumpy in their tracks, and to make them look around for even a moment, is what I try to achieve in my lobbies.

At Haymarket, there is a Tony Cragg sculpture, delicious in its mercuryness, taking centre stage. It plays tricks on the eye – is it falling to the floor or rising from the ground? Everybody sees something different in this sculpture – some see faces, some see smoke and mirrors – but it is all in the eye of the beholder.

Art in my home and hotel bedrooms is altogether another opportunity to hang whatever I please. I once joked to a friend that if she stood still long enough I could make her into a standing lamp or if you left a handkerchief in front of me I would frame it and hang it on the wall. It is often about the framing as much as the art that makes a wall visually interesting.

Collections of items are always fun – in Refuel at the Soho Hotel, we collected old oil cans and containers, adding in dinky toys, to make a boyish montage. A large collection of similar objects, like plates, evenly placed against a good colour wall looks great; several paintings by the same artist hung at one end of the room and finished off at the other end of the room with another piece by the same artist gives the space balance.

Do not feel that art has to be wildly expensive. I use some expensive pieces in a jaw-dropping way, but at home I truly prefer the work of young artists, and work that has no value except that it has a bit of heart. Art has become a commodity, and I know one dealer who has copies of famous works on his walls and the real thing hidden away in a safe. How mad is that?

PREVIOUS PAGE:
Striped fabric by Pierre Frey used on the chapter opening number and a close-up of the Crosby's Plensa sculpture.

OPPOSITE:
The old oil cans and containers at Refuel.

PREVIOUS PAGE:

Aphrodite presides over the Soho drawing room, providing a focal point for the room as the windows behind become her frame. The embroidered fabric on the bergères to her left are covered in an embroidered, boiled wool design that was inspired by the fabric of an old knitting bag.

OPPOSITE:

Hanging a large painting in the centre of a collection of similar smaller paintings ensures the smaller ones feel more important and don't get lost on the wall.

ABOVE:

Botero's 10-foot-tall bronze cat at the Soho had to be installed before the ground floor was built and the building and interior had to work around him in all his grandness. We even placed a long comfy floor cushion on one of the lobby steps for people to sit on and admire him. He is a mighty soul of a sculpture.

OPPOSITE:

A drawing of one Lyn Chadwick's sculptural ideas hangs in a clever frame where the dragging black lines around it draws the eye in.

ABOVE:

An Alan Jones painting sits above a collection of cardboard cows on the top of a painted orange sixties' sideboard. It's a weird but arresting combination.

The enormous height of the Crosby Bar's ceilings meant I had to think of overscaling the pictures. There is an eight-foot bull, two very large oil paintings by Joe Fan, a collection of vintage, plastic pendant lights, a couple of Asafo flags, some fairground insects in metal and a large Senufo carving of a bird, plus our own installation of old fifties' telephones that I bought from Alex Randall. Oh yes, and four charming cardboard collages of a smiling Queen in spring, summer, autumn and winter, wearing wonderful flowery hats and drop earrings from Mimi in Biarritz.

OVERLEAF:
Two very large oil paintings by Joe Fan bought from the Thackeray Gallery.

I love large spaces that let art breathe. In the basement at Soho we have a series of paintings by the wonderful Sandra Blow. She was a pocket-handkerchief-sized woman who looked a little like Mary Quant with kohl-rimmed eyes and the most vibrant personality. One of my most treasured memories is of the artist Craigie Aitchison and Sandra Blow sitting either side of the fireplace in Soho's drawing room discussing life in general. Both are sadly no longer with us, and greatly missed by the art world.

PREVIOUS PAGE:

A Mark Entwisle triptych bought because it reminded me of one of my daughters swimming in the Serpentine.

ABOVE:

A series of miniature mannequins relate to the rest of the drawing room at Knightsbridge by being hand-painted to match the fabrics and paintings in the room.

OPPOSITE:

The top of a weathervane sits in a base made from an old piece of driftwood with two metal fox doorstops attached at either end. The base of the stem is surrounded by a collection of shells from the Sahara.

In the drawing room at Charlotte Street, it is the Bloomsbury-inspired curtains, rugs and cushions, tailor-made for the room, which become the art collection.

ABOVE:

A Duncan Grant painting contrasts against the contemporary 'Harlequin' fabric by Edit.

OPPOSITE:

A Graham Fransella painting sits behind a collection of stone balls and round sculptural face. We have another fabulous Fransella that hangs in the entrance hall of the Knightsbridge – one day Graham rang me from Australia and I thought he was going to say how much he loved the way we had displayed his work; in fact, he was ringing to say we'd hung it sideways. I am afraid I am a true decorator at heart, and hung it because of the dimension and shape in the space. I hope I am forgiven.

A collection of Alfred Wolmark paintings, in their original, early twentieth-century frames, hang alongside paintings by Vanessa Bell and Duncan Grant. This combination of art from the same period looks very strong together, especially against the simplicity of a natural linen-lined wall.

ABOVE:

ABOVE:

This black and white room is suddenly given lots of impact with a contemporary collage by Sandra Blow. The room would be less significant without it; the painting helps to finish it off.

PREVIOUS PAGE:

Collections of decorative jugs and racks of antique plates.

OPPOSITE:

We commissioned Martin Richman via Louise Hallet to make a very large light installation for the swimming pool area at the Haymarket. The idea was to bring life into the large basement area; the inspiration was to watch the light rising on the horizon in lines of varying colour.

I like putting pictures in front of bookcases – here, Carey Mortimer's tempura paintings frame the entrance to a panelled room.

These multi-media collage artworks by Jack Milroy and Anselm Kiefer
lend a moody edge to the lobby space at Crosby Street.
The piece by Kiefer (right) took six men to heave into place.

The orange and black of the Callum Innes painting at the end of the lobby captivates the eye, helping to provide a perfect point to end your view – it frames the room, especially where there are areas around it that drift off.

My original idea of 'art inspired by the written word' was the catalyst for purchasing this very large Jaume Plensa head sculpture. I like that it is see-through as I didn't want a hunking, heavy piece in this position, but instead one that was there but not there. Children love to scramble under and into it, bringing endless joy and fun to this lobby space.

OPPOSITE:

Works by Craigie Aitchison and Nicola Clark hang beside two decorated shields from New Guinea. It's an odd combination that makes a captivating corner.

ABOVE:

An old painting of a great big boat in a man's study lends the room an escapist feel.

ABOVE:

A friend's test match cricket ball and set of bails have been positioned on Astro Turf and framed in perspex.

LEFT:

A framed illustration of W.G. Grace, one of cricket's key innovators and recognised as one's of the sport's greatest players, hangs in the restaurant.

Dorset Square was the site of the first Lord's cricket ground in London, in fact, little squares of turf from the square's gardens opposite the hotel are still sent to cricket pitches all around the world. Here, we've had fun with using various cricket memorabilia throughout the hotel's interiors scheme.

ABOVE, CLOCKWISE:

An old cricket bat is given a Mondrian-style makeover. Elsewhere in the hotel, we had fun covering various bats with different papers and fabrics to give them added interest.

A large framed display of old and used cricket bats hangs in a hallway.

A close-up of a ball used in a large wall collage which we've hung on one of the walls in the restaurant. It's background is pages taken from old Wisden Cricketers' Almanacks. The ball here inspired us to create door knobs for all the hotel's rooms from old cricket balls.

A detail of an old school locker, used to house crockery in the restaurant.

Taking Risks

When I talk about 'taking risks', I think I mean 'not being predictable' rather than tempting disastrous fate. I see so many rooms that look as if they have been painted by numbers, or pieces of furniture bought simply because they have a trendy designer name attached to them. In my opinion, this simply makes for interiors that are safe and uninteresting.

I don't start by thinking 'how can I risk doing this' because I don't like rooms that are gimmicky or too adulterated. It is finding the right balance between adding a few extra pieces and maintaining the line of a room that pleases the eye. I like my rooms to last. If the bones are good then they will go on forever. That's why wood panelling and books will always be favourites – but that is not to say there can't be light in the book cases created with illuminated strips and a library ladder of glowing perspex and metal.

I have been creating living spaces for quite a long time now and the concept of taking risks is not as frightening to me anymore. I bought some reclaimed hand-painted strips of wood that were old and falling to pieces but I loved the painting on them and the splintery look of the hard wood. I hung them in strips around a room and overlaid them with paintings and pictures when they looked too raggedy. To suit this home-made mood, I sewed felt scenes on the upholstery of the chairs and found remnants of fabrics to make into cushions and to cover the sofa. I was always a demon on the sewing machine when was I was young (luckily I now have a fab little team to help me pull it all together) – but the essence is still the same now, as it was then. I love to see someone's personality in a room. Don't be afraid to show it.

At the moment I am designing a fabric on linen that will have a hazy, rubbed-out stripe, overlaid with a tangle of willow-type leaves, overlaid with a darker vine, overlaid with a cut-out collage of an African print. I think this might be taking a risk. It's a mixture of delicacy and strength, yet simplicity and a dab of singing colour too… which is also the recipe for a perfect room.

PREVIOUS PAGE:
Woven lattice-work leather by Dedar used on the chapter opening number; pieces commissioned for the CAA 'A Living Space' exhibition, including work by artists Sarah-Jane Selwood, Rupert Spira, Malcolm Martin and Gaynor Dowling, and Alison Crowther.

OPPOSITE:
Commissioned plates for the same exhibition.

I am afraid that I am not a purist. I think it a lovely thing to be but it's just that there are so many opportunities and so many talented people to use that being a purist would constrain me in a box. It would be like only wearing navy and beige all your life. Just too tasteful for words.

OPPOSITE:

Ikat weaves by Mary Restieaux sit framed above an Edward Teasdale reclaimed driftwood cabinet.

In 2010 I was asked by Contemporary Applied Arts to curate
an exhibition using all their 200 members to make a living
space using their arts and crafts, to help give ideas to people
about incorporating bespoke pieces into their home. Firstly,
I had to think of an accessible way to involve all the members
and came up with the idea of asking each one to make a
10-inch plate. It didn't matter if their medium was ceramic,
wood, fabric, silver, knitting, or paint – they could do whatever
they wanted. It was so exciting when the plates started to
arrive as they were all so different, each one so individual.
Hanging them together instantly created a feast for the eyes
and a celebration of unique lines of thought and presentation.

Putting together these disparate pieces was taking a
risk but it was fun. It was exciting and inspiring,
and most importantly, it worked.

For my own contribution, I created a very individual space
that started with the inspiration of Breon O'Casey's paintings
and colouring. I asked him if we could recreate two of his
paintings, with the help of The Rug Company, with one of a
dove as a woven hanging, the other of a tree on a woollen
carpet. Pippa Caley made a sofa for us using boiled wools in
tones of soft grey and embroidered it in her own special way;
Michelle House created hand-painted blinds in an abstract
design as a backdrop for some wonderful ceramics; and there
was lots of wood, in different colours and varieties by artists
such as Ashley Cartwright and Jim Partridge, including a floor-
to-ceiling chest of drawers in ash and oak and a wavy screen
from Alison Crowther.

Bold, arresting colour combinations, textures and trims lends the drawing room at Number Sixteen maximum impact.

The details pull it together: Muuto pendant lights shed a subtle glow on the dark paintwork; striped curtains and vivid yellow or a dash of magenta fabric as upholstery add drama; and the zigzag trim, piping and tassels are perfect finishing touches on sofas and chairs. Always use real books.

If you're surrounded by something interesting, it immediately gets the brainbox working in an entirely different way.

The harmony in the room is created by making the black tonal – from the darker tones on the sofa to the softer greys of the hand-blocked and printed Marthe Armitage wallpaper, teamed with a pale rug and muted painted purple ceiling – and then giving it punches of colour in the fabric, coffee tables and lights. Think about your framing.

A walking tour through the Haymarket Hotel:
A Lesson in Adventure

Although each of the following rooms has a different feel, I spent a lot of time and thought on finding a way to unify them in almost imperceptible ways (like threading through a common element such as colour, material or artist). I was very conscious that I wanted each room to run harmoniously into the other.

From the bright yellow, black and silver-hued lobby at Haymarket Hotel, this chair in a flamboyant Moroccan fabric ends the journey in yellow. A Sandra Blow painting hangs behind, catching your eye and carrying you around the corner and into a calming conservatory-style space, with its flood of light and the garden-like palette of blue, green and grey.

Christopher Farr's Carnival fabric on chairs and cushions teams with driftwood pendants and Paul Winstanley's 'Veil 25' painting, which feels like looking out onto a scene through sixties' net curtains.

Dynamic pieces of art are brilliant in a space like this where there is no access to windows because, in actual fact, the painting itself becomes like looking out of the window at a view.

OPPOSITE:

A piece by Jack Milroy showing a macabre view of skulls underground – it is very unexpected to find such a piece against such a highly patterned backdrop, and yet it is infinitely more interesting here than on a plain wall.

ABOVE:

A maiden table, fashioned from a single piece of oak, designed by Russell Pinch for Benchmark.

The most important task for this room was to have its own sense of arrival. It couldn't just
feel like a passageway, en route from the conservatory into the Shooting Gallery. It had to
stand out on its own, but I didn't fight its lack of access to natural light and its lower ceilings;
instead, I had a lot of fun playing with a patchwork mix of indigos, denims and reds to make it
feel cosy and comforting, the perfect private space for guests to relax.

I like people, I want them to be comfortable. I like design that
is inclusive, so that it doesn't matter who you are, you don't
feel left out. I am happiest when I come into a room like this
and see that people have moved things around.

Sofas covered in an embroidered squiggle fabric by Chelsea Textiles. The ottoman is made from a piece of antique fabric trimmed with leather rope from Andrew Martin. On the side table, a broken marble bust and an abstract painting, inspired by ripples made by water on sand, provide a fantastic focal point to the room.

The pièce de résistance, the building's iconic Shooting Gallery, lies at the end of this visual journey. Here, this vast room with eighteen-foot-high ceilings (which was historically used for shooting practice in the 1800s by countrymen visiting the city), is the perfect backdrop for a dramatic de Gournay sepia-hued wallpaper, exotic art by Oliver Messel and unexpected touches like a seventies lucite table and sixties' lamps by Rougier. I wanted it to create a neutral background so the people using the space would stand out within it.

Too much is never too much. I've always found that bedrooms with eaves feel less pokey if you wallpaper all over – it gets rid of difficult lines and somehow makes it feel bigger. Paper from Brunschwig & Fils and zebra rug from Habitat.

In a central hallway, leading to a kitchen, a wrought-iron chandelier is customised with brass cooking implements to make it fit with its environment and yet feel unique. The ceramic sculpture on the table was made by an old friend and lends a humanity to the space.

Four vivid-print handkerchiefs by Peter Adler are imaginatively framed to add life and impact.

framing is important – I like to frame things in such a way that the illustration looks more striking and stands its ground in a room.

Living With The Things You Love

Every home has its own spirit. It can be such a joy to walk through your own front door and leave the outside world behind. I love the unusual things found in the home, like a row of saddles left on the upstairs landing, or the Himalayan yogurt-maker found somewhere on a trip abroad. Gardens keep on growing but interiors die if they are not loved and the door is kept closed for too long.

I am not interested in the designer chair or immaculately covered sofa – it is who is sitting in the chair, where there is the right spot to read the newspaper on a dull day, or the best space to eat toast and look at the birds outside the window. The meaning of home to me is about the kitchen mostly, and mealtimes with family and friends.

I love my children, but I don't want to cover every surface with silver frames of them, so I end up putting photographs in front of the spines of books on a row of bookshelves. It looks more interesting. If your husband likes making flies for fishing, give him a lovely place to do it in a good light by the kitchen table, so everyone can feel involved. Having said that, it's probably not a good idea to paint the whole house in Arsenal football colours because it is his team of choice. There always has to be give and take.

I love a busy, colourful room with layers of handiwork and art, but these have to be tempered with another space that is more zen-like and calm. They complement each other and give space between the frivolity. I have my yoga room at the top of the house with a skylight to see the clouds passing by.

The things I love are also about escapism and dipping into the imagination. We have the gypsy caravan in the garden. I think I will retire there. There is a bed and everything is within reach without having to get up. I can have tea and biscuits without moving an inch. It's the perfect antidote to everyday life.

PREVIOUS PAGE:
A detail of a favourite Indian embroidery used on the chapter opening number, and a detail of the gypsy caravan.

OPPOSITE:
The family's gypsy caravan nestled in the garden.

In my daughter Min's room, the way the Cornish artist Judy Buxton dabs on quite a bit of oil paint to her paintings gives a stronger presence than a watercolour, and the yellow echoes beautifully with the colour of the old desk (which sits higher than usual so I teamed it with a stool rather than a chair). The hot-pink phone gives a fabulous splash of Barbie.

My personal style signifier is my jewellery. I tend to always have some statement piece on, possibly more than one at a time. I like the work of Ayala Bar who uses fabrics, stitching and strange little bits of *passementerie*. They add that little twist.

A special place at home, to rest and relax, is in front of the dressing table in my bedroom – I have used an old Indian embroidered border, sewn onto a piece of creamy linen, to cover a kitchen table (a close-up of this is pictured overleaf), and it has all my mad, colourful gypsy necklaces, a mirror, jars of cream and it provides a good space to write letters and cards.

One of my wallpaper designs of scattered flowers used in a bathroom.

ABOVE:

Under a painting by Scottish artist John Boyd sits a deep-buttoned bedroom chair.

OPPOSITE:

Tiffany's room is an enveloping mix of warm reds and a mix of fabrics – including a patchwork throw on the bed which she made herself from a mass of old fabric samples.

A fabric picture by Anna Raymond takes centre stage, flanked by two old rusticating mirrors either side of the old French fireplace to give the impression of space and depth. Modern Brutalist lamp bases add another dimension to the scheme. Sometimes you want plainness on the outside and the centre to be detailed, so the white on walls here works to offset the colour from the paintings and fabrics on the chairs and sofas.

A side table made from reclaimed metalwork on aluminium legs and a marble top contrasts with a very modern, welded metal chair.

Hair pins found on a trip to Africa, mounted on perspex, and a small sculpture found at a Royal Academy Summer Exhibition bring an inquisitive detail to the top of the mantelpiece.

RIGHT:
Carol Sinclair pebbles in a concrete base with Linda Bird pots, on top of a shagreen coffee table.

It's the collection of pictures on the wall, including an exaggerated painting of a seagull found on a trip to Monhegan Island, off the coast of Maine, that really makes this room cosy and interesting. Voyage Russian-style fabrics were used with red suede piping on an old French chair and a Surrealist face fabric for the headboard and valance.

This marquetry *escritoire* is the perfect place for pictures of the children and Granny, a showy little piece that makes the most of a rather gloomy corner space, and it's the first thing you see when you come into the bedroom.

HILDA BRENT

I have had this picture of Hilda Brent for many years – she must have been some kind of leading lady. When I look at it I always think, 'go for it Hilda, you're no shrinking violet'. She's going to go around with me forever **– it always makes me think, if she can do it, I can do it too.**

Acknowledgements

With great thanks to the fantastic, inspiring and wonderful team who helped bring this book together: Craig Markham, Kate Pollard at Hardie Grant, Simon Brown, David Eldridge at Two Associates and Fiona McCarthy who made my written word make sense and made me laugh. Tim, Tiffany, Willow and Min Kemp for being my sternest critics and all my working team, especially the builders, curtain- and furniture-makers and picture-framers, and everyone in my studio.

First published in 2012 by Hardie Grant Books

Hardie Grant Books (UK)
5th & 6th Floors
52-54 Southwalk Street
LONDON SE1 1RU, UK
www.hardiegrant.co.uk

Hardie Grant Books (Australia)
Ground Floor, Building 1
658 Church Street
Melbourne, VIC 3121
www.hardiegrant.com.au

The moral rights of Kit Kemp to be identified as the author of this work have been asserted by her in accordance with the Copyright, Designs and Patents Act 1988.

All rights reserved. No part of this publication may be reproduced, stored in a retrieval system or transmitted in any form by any means, electronic, electrostatic, magnetic tape, mechanical, photocopying, recording or otherwise, without the prior written permission of the Publisher.

British Library Cataloguing-in-Publication Data. A catalogue record for this book is available from the British Library.

ISBN 978-1-74270-393-0

Commissioning Editor: Kate Pollard
Cover and internal design: Two Associates
Photography: Simon Brown
Inside Out, page 73 – photography of view outside Crosby Street Hotel window by Annie Schlechter
(www.annieschlechter.com)
Compare & Contrast, page 129 – photograph of Mona Lisa with sunglasses by Martyn Thompson
(www.martynthompsonstudio.com)

Every attempt has been made to contact copyright holders. The publishers would like to hear from any copyright holders who may not have been attributed.

Colour reproduction: by XY Digital Limited, London
Printed and bound China by 1010 Printing International Limited

10 9 8 7

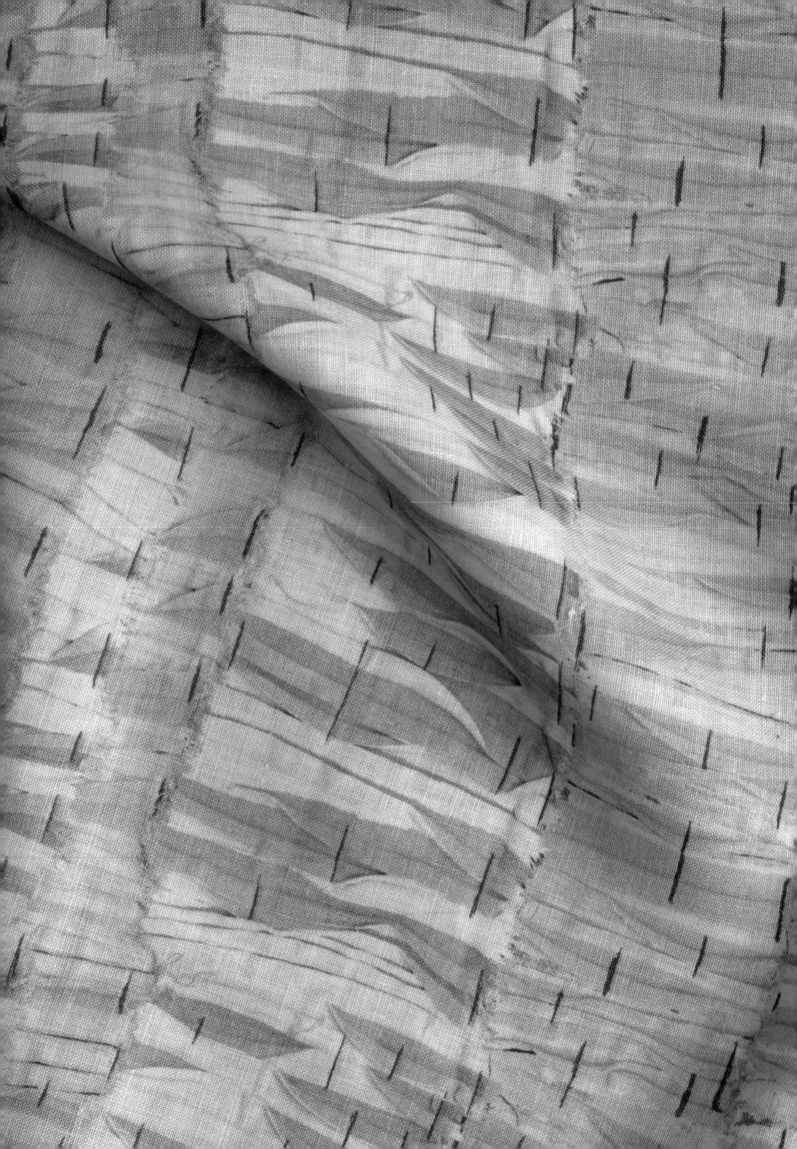